Dec 2017

D0890156

Kansas City, MO Public Library
0000185517000

First Drawings
Aircraft

BIG BUDDY
FIRST DRAWINGS
BOOKS

Big Buddy Books
An Imprint of Abdo Publishing
abdopublishing.com

By Katie Lajiness

abdopublishing.com

Published by Abdo Publishing, a division of ABDO, PO Box 398166, Minneapolis, Minnesota 55439.
Copyright © 2017 by Abdo Consulting Group, Inc. International copyrights reserved in all countries. No part
of this book may be reproduced in any form without written permission from the publisher. Big Buddy Books™
is a trademark and logo of Abdo Publishing.

Printed in the United States of America, North Mankato, Minnesota.
092016
012017

THIS BOOK CONTAINS
RECYCLED MATERIALS

Illustrations: Michael Jacobsen/Spectrum Studio
Interior Photos: Deposit Photos

Coordinating Series Editor: Tamara L. Britton
Graphic Design: Taylor Higgins, Maria Hosley

Publisher's Cataloging-in-Publication Data

Names: Lajiness, Katie, author.
Title: Aircraft / by Katie Lajiness.
Description: Minneapolis, MN : Abdo Publishing, 2017. | Series: First drawings |
     Includes index.
Identifiers: LCCN 2016944886 | ISBN 9781680785197 (lib. bdg.) |
     ISBN 9781680798791 (ebook)
Subjects: LCSH: Airplanes in art--Juvenile literature. | Space vehicles in art--
     Juvenile literature. | Drawing--Technique--Juvenile literature.
Classification: DDC 743/.8962913334--dc23
LC record available at http://lccn.loc.gov/2016944886

Table of Contents

Getting Started 4

Adding Color 6

Blimp 8

Cargo Plane 12

Helicopter 16

Passenger Plane 20

Fighter Jet 24

On Your Own 30

Glossary 31

Websites 31

Index 32

Getting Started

Today, you're going to draw aircraft. Not sure you know how to draw? Aircraft are easy to **sketch** if you break them down into circles, ovals, rectangles, squares, and triangles.

To begin, you'll need paper, a sharpened pencil, a big eraser, and a flat surface. Draw each shape lightly. When these **guidelines** are light, it is easy to erase and try again.

BASIC SHAPES   Circle   Oval   Rectangle   Square   Triangle

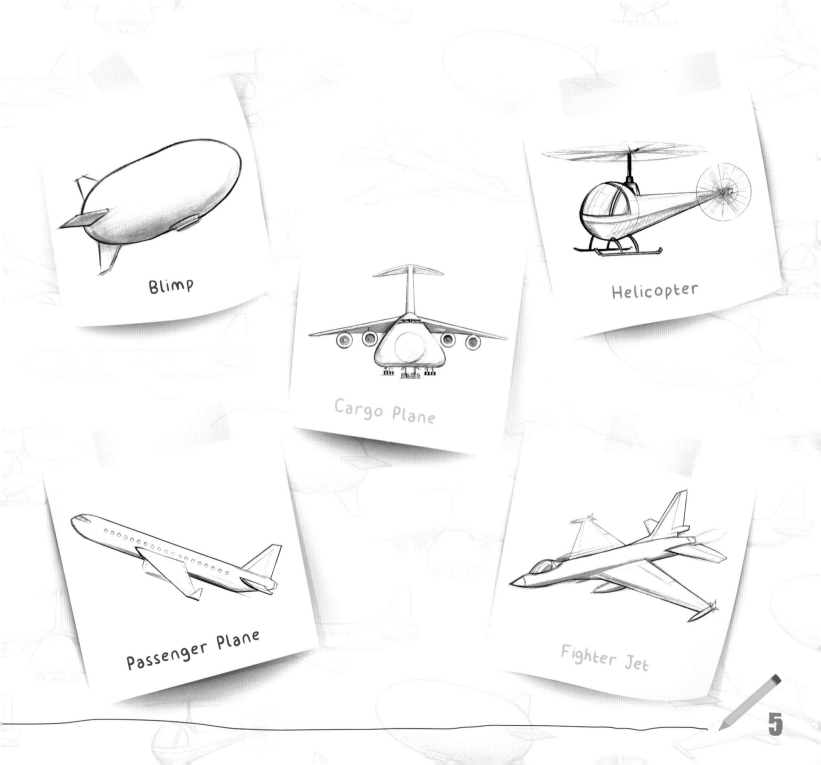

Blimp

Cargo Plane

Helicopter

Passenger Plane

Fighter Jet

5

Adding Color

Once you learn to draw an object, you may want to add color. Let's learn how to mix colors and add shading.

Shading

MARKERS
Use similar colors to create shading.

PENCILS AND CRAYONS
Use less pressure for lighter shades and more pressure for darker shades.

PAINTS
Add white to lighten and black or blue to darken shades.

There are three primary colors. They are red, yellow, and blue. These colors cannot be made by mixing other colors. However, you can make many colors by mixing primary colors together.

Color mixing

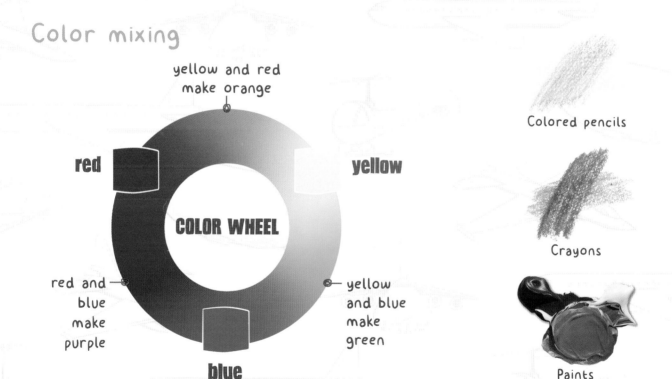

yellow and red make orange

red

yellow

COLOR WHEEL

red and blue make purple

yellow and blue make green

blue

Colored pencils

Crayons

Paints

Tip Create **contrast** by using colors from opposite ends of the color wheel.

Blimp

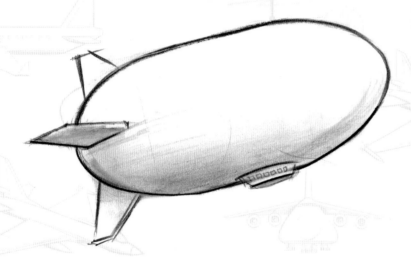

Let's learn to draw a blimp!

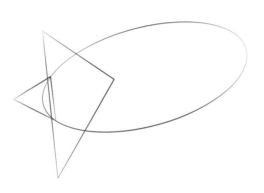

Draw basic oval and triangle **guidelines** for the body, rudder, and elevator.

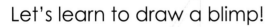

Erase guidelines
once you have
the parts drawn.

STEP 2

Connect the shapes to form the blimp's **outline**.

STEP 3

Sketch an oval **guideline** at the bottom of the blimp for the cabin.

Erase guidelines
once you have
the parts drawn.

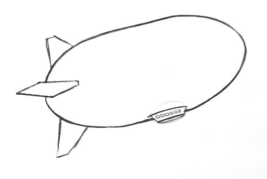

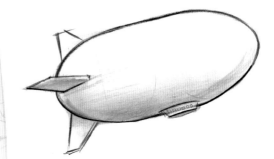

STEP **4**

Add windows to your
blimp's cabin.

STEP **5**

Create **texture** and shape by
adding shading to your blimp.

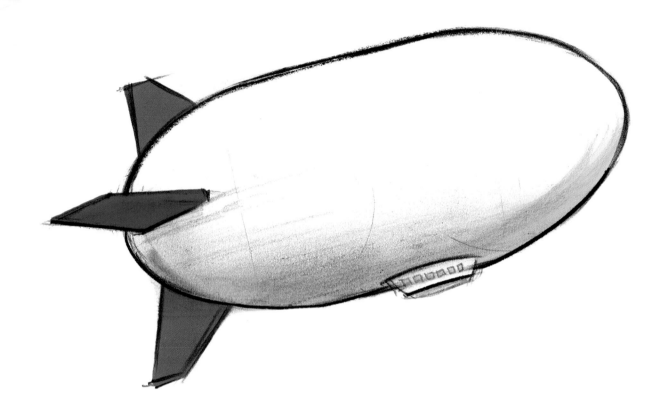

It's time for some color! You can add your own color and shading to personalize your drawing.

YOU DID IT!

Bravo! You drew a blimp.

Cargo Plane

Let's learn to draw a cargo plane!

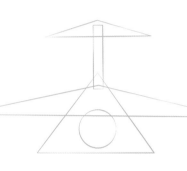

Draw basic triangle, circle, and rectangle **guidelines** for the body, wings, and tail.

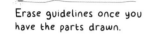

Erase guidelines once you
have the parts drawn.

Connect the shapes to form
the **outline**.

Draw the plane's engines. Now
add **details** to the wing and tail.

13

Draw the plane's wheels and windows.

Create **texture** and **depth** by adding shading to your cargo plane.

YOU DID IT!

Well done!
You drew
a cargo
plane.

STEP 6

It's time for some color! You can
add your own color and shading to
personalize your drawing.

Helicopter

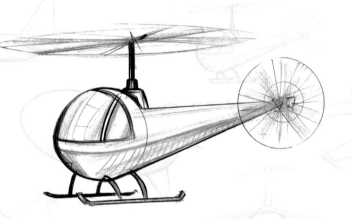

Let's learn to draw a helicopter!

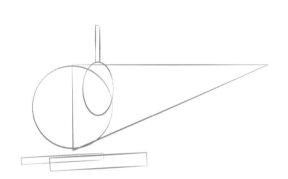

Draw basic circle, triangle, oval, and rectangle **guidelines** for the cockpit, tail, shaft, and landing skids.

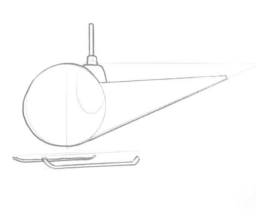

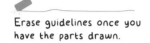

Erase guidelines once you
have the parts drawn.

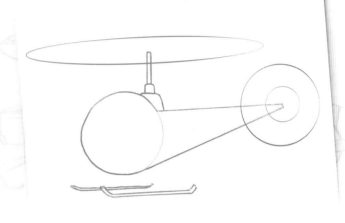

STEP 2

Connect the shapes to form the helicopter's **outline**.

STEP 3

Sketch an oval and circle for the helicopter's rotors.

17

STEP 4

Fill in the helicopter's windows and finish the landing skids.

STEP 5

Add **details** to make the rotor blades. Create **texture** and shape by adding shading to your helicopter.

YOU DID IT!

Congratulations! You drew a helicopter.

STEP 6

It's time for some color! You can add your own color and shading to personalize your drawing.

Passenger Plane

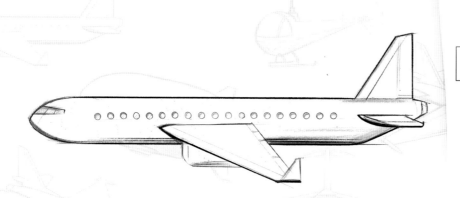

Let's learn to draw a
passenger plane!

Draw basic rectangle and triangle
guidelines for the plane's body,
wings, and tail.

20

Erase guidelines once you
have the parts drawn.

STEP 2

Connect the shapes to form the
plane's **outline**.

STEP 3

Draw **guidelines** for your
plane's windows.

Erase guidelines once you have the parts drawn.

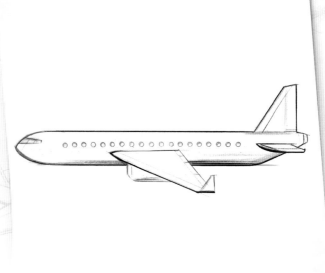

STEP 4

Add **details** by drawing circles and straight lines for windows. Draw an engine under the wing.

STEP 5

Create **texture** and shape by adding shading to your plane.

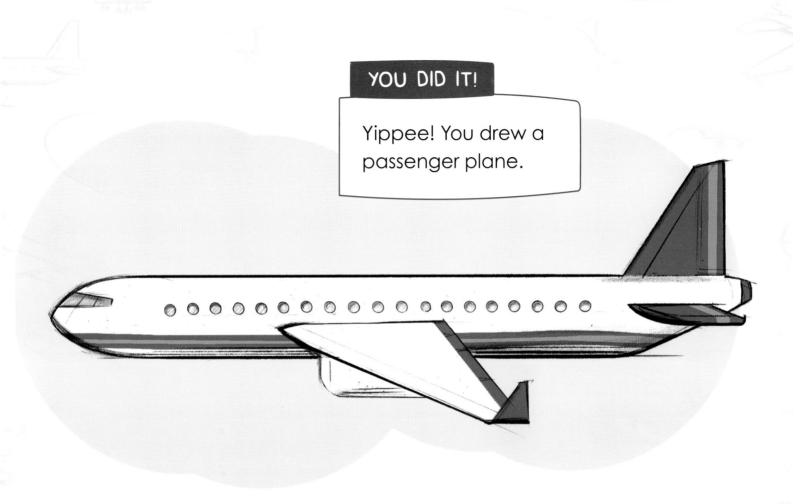

YOU DID IT!

Yippee! You drew a passenger plane.

STEP **6**

It's time for some color! You can add your own color and shading to personalize your drawing.

Fighter Jet

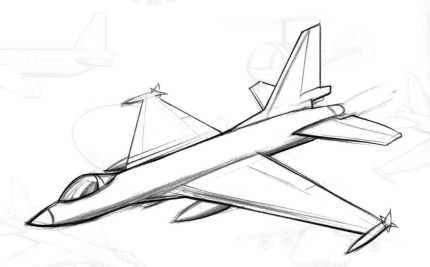

Let's learn to draw a fighter jet!

Draw a basic rectangle **guideline** for the fighter jet's body.

Erase guidelines once you
have the parts drawn.

Shape the rectangle to form the
jet's main **outline**.

Sketch triangles as **guidelines**
for the wings and tail.

Erase guidelines once you
have the parts drawn.

Shape the jet's wings and tail.

Create new oval and triangle
guidelines for the cockpit and
tail fin.

Erase guidelines once you
have the parts drawn.

STEP 6

Shape the cockpit and tail fin.
Add a divider to the cockpit.

STEP 7

Draw missiles on the wing tips
and under the wings.

It's time to add **details** to the wings and tail fin.

Create **texture** and shape by adding shading.

Tools There are many tools you can use to add color such as crayons, colored pencils, paints, or markers.

It's time for some color! You can add your own color and shading to personalize your drawing.

YOU DID IT!

Yay! You drew a fighter jet.

On Your Own

To build your drawing skills, practice finding basic shapes in everyday objects. Finding basic shapes can help you draw almost anything. Use what you've learned to draw other aircraft. The more you draw, the better you will be!

Glossary

contrast the amount of difference in color or brightness.

depth measurement from top to bottom or from front to back.

detail a minor decoration, such as a cat's whiskers.

guideline a rule or instruction that shows or tells how something should be done.

outline the outer edges of a shape.

sketch to make a rough drawing.

texture the look or feel of something.

Websites

To learn more about First Drawings, visit **booklinks.abdopublishing.com**. These links are routinely monitored and updated to provide the most current information available.

Index

aircraft features **8, 9, 10, 12, 13, 14, 16, 17, 18, 20, 21, 22, 24, 25, 26, 27, 28**

basic shapes **4, 8, 9, 12, 13, 16, 17, 20, 21, 22, 24, 25, 26, 30**

blimp **5, 8, 9, 10, 11**

cargo plane **5, 12, 13, 14, 15**

color **6, 7, 11, 15, 19, 23, 28, 29**

contrast **7**

crayon **6, 28**

eraser **4, 9, 10, 13, 17, 21, 22, 25, 26, 27**

fighter jet **5, 24, 25, 26, 27, 28, 29**

flat surface **4**

helicopter **5, 16, 17, 18, 19**

marker **6, 28**

paint **6, 28**

paper **4**

passenger plane **5, 20, 21, 22, 23**

pencil **4, 6, 28**

shading **6, 10, 11, 14, 15, 18, 19, 22, 23, 28, 29**